COMFORT

COMFORT

Sarah Heady

SPUYTEN DUYVIL
New York City

Thank you to the editors of the following journals in which some of these poems appeared previously, at times in slightly different form: *Actual Favorite Meadow*; *AMERARCANA: A Bird & Beckett Review*; *Elderly*; *FENCE*; *Ghost Proposal*; *HOLD: A Journal*; *Jewish Currents*; *OmniVerse*; and *where is the river :: a poetry experiment*. Thank you to Kristy Bowen, editor of dancing girl press, for publishing *Corduroy Road* (2021), a chapbook that contains the conceptual seeds of *Comfort* and several of its poems.

© 2022 Sarah Heady
ISBN 978-1-952419-77-5

Cover image by Clare Rojas
Untitled, 2005, latex and gouache on wooden panels

Library of Congress Cataloging-in-Publication Data

Names: Heady, Sarah, author.
Title: Comfort / Sarah Heady.
Description: New York City : Spuyten Duyvil, [2022].
Identifiers: LCCN 2021032354 | ISBN 9781952419775 (paperback)
Classification: LCC PS3608.E23525 C66 2022 | DDC 811/.6--dc23/eng/20211028
LC record available at https://lccn.loc.gov/2021032354

to Joe
for being there when I came home

CONTENTS

: sunup :	1
: day :	25
: dusk :	55
: acknowledgments :	89
: notes :	93

If only she'd known then what comfort was coming, she'd have spared herself a little.

Marilynne Robinson

Edges in the landscape are always lessons waiting to be learned.

William Wyckoff

Better than fecundity are lists.

Elizabeth Robinson

i do not go to bed wishing for brown or red sleep, i will accept what kind becomes me

: *SUNUP* :

like a call collect

sun enters :

assuming permission

                      asking forgiveness later

                                          revivified
                                                  dirt with water

                                          revivified
                                                plains with ocean

slip me one. i was a slip once :

a cinch purse   of green sea

    glass   tiny bible

    splinter of wood from boston

    grain of atlantic sand

is a tight little island, a prairie zephyr, a hoax, an average western type, is a pile of rope, pig-iron, coke, softwood, hardwood, bran & jam-stained fingers right in the time-spot, ticks in the fur. is apple peel auguries, weevils in flour. twenty-four prunes with senna leaves, one pint of boiling water, a plug of wood covered in flannel & double-fleshed by corrosion. is in mourning black & gingham, buckwheat, greengage, mackerel in kits & layers of raisins. is drums of figs instead of hard, ungainly knobs. does not project too far beyond the general outline, affords a concealed recess for the fingers : the latter greater than it appears, & still more so in nebraska a package of words delivered whole

& crisp, a skirt in wind :

baby   i hope you've packed your bags

already   else we're in for the trip

of our brief   hard lifetimes   wearing

like scarves

the tripe of grown cows

(we all ran away
from the same thing

not *toward*

which was the kind of movement
i loved until

we stopped here)

is a hook, a hood, a helpmeet, a platform, a seeder, an arrow through topsoil saying *come* : is flax into bales, into rope, into twine, sacks, paper from straw, glass, starch, starch from maize, wheat, &c., canned fruits, potted meats, vegetables, blankets, woolens, carpets (cheap carpets), leathers & skins. how so many flourish in a place so young is quite a mystery to me : a can of lye dissolved in a gallon of rainwater, ten cents' worth of salts & all scraps dried, all scraps rolled up fine & streaked : a cupful of spirits to each pail, each revenant caravan : a cloud of smoke that somehow brays : braided hair in a frame, seeds for the eyes : a single continuous effort : is white squares tatted, mended, starched : quarry for swimming, colony of two : from sod to hardwood, if you're lucky : salamander bricks in a stack by the tractors. vision is white lines that come from the eyes themselves : projections across the plain :

bodies
hunker into orbits
as shoulders
in sockets must be
yanked out to feel
anything

flags with
no real insignia
only shoddy patches   covering something
now invisible :

                      an economy

founded on chains of proximity that ceased to exist decades ago

      some stand in a line   forging swords
      others circle the house   building domes

      of breath about it   saying let's start

over in english :
language
of second chances

                                      land running

                              & running until its fever
                              finally breaks at the sea

        & you running alongside long enough
        to cut the remainders off with faith

is waiting for the mails. is disappointed wishing they'd write more often. is seeing the ghost of the fence. is mending until plum midnight. is three nights setting a bucket of water on the bedroom floor to collect miasmas. is exhausted, entirely worn away. is making the best of & making the beds. is scratching along the riverbed for finds : from buckshot to walnuts, submergence, emergence : *i therefore desire more solid comfort* : agate, cornelian, jasper, alluvial soil. is roaming the pomological fair, pressing into the skins. is detecting a thickness to the season. is checking future wind with saplings, measuring winter minima. is all sunsets & auroras & how much farther westward he is not prepared to say : the drift, the lacustrine, or loess, alluvium : puzzles : colored pictures or pieces of pictures : catarrh & lumbago, falling of the womb : oval, oblong, obvate, abruptly pointed in a short, close cluster : we have no connection whatever with any other company : dried currants, eggs repacked : putty in bladders & batten per linear foot. oxien was, and still is, the only true food for the nerves. it ranges in thickness : perfectly homogenous, exposed, rubbed fine, the size of a shot : *COMFORT* : "the key to a million and a quarter homes" : a strengthener & a friend to women : a truly formidable list

household notes

sulphur & molasses to purify
blood   for cough a poultice
of bread & milk   or bacon rind
& manure   in a little bag hung
about the neck   or kerosene-
-soaked red flannel over the throat
(or onions)   in case
of summer complaint   boil
blackberries for children   to cure
bilious headache drink juice   drink
charcoal   a teaspoon of
ammonia added once
a week will make the house grow

building the barn :

balloon frame *ting*

rings out over space :

a cage to float away

bugs vibrate, weighty

summer after

summer after

summer after

& to paint

our farmhouse orange

we harvested sugar

pumpkins

we needed all twelve

children to get enough

gallons for the kitchen

ell alone

villages tumble out of crossroads :
the season's decay so soon
they must begin right now and not
let up :

workers hooked by the arm in contra
or square dance look each other
over for signs of sterility

womb plumbed : a churn for making

humans out of loneliness

i think that one cannot take a farm hap-hazard in the bottom, as he might do in some of the table-lands : i think it will not be without interest : i think it will not be difficult for a stranger to travel alone & i think of the woman said to be a seer : her grave cordoned off on its own the far side of the cemetery : a chain around her collecting coins & candle stubs from the locally curious & i think about the baby (little stranger) on its way to getting baptized : thrown from the buggy & buried alone by the tree-line apart from the other saved souls because it never got wet. this map may be taken as accurate as far as it goes & whoever intends to make a new home in this new country will find it of very great value :

i forget what a new friend feels like   (our place on the small hill)

when women first came here it might be months

before they heard another woman's voice

but sunup is respiteless,

constant :

REQUESTS

Will someone send me a few old COMFORTS, of the days of Aunt Minerva. Will return favor any way I can.

MISS BEATRICE SMITH, Cleveland, Va.

Would like to have the sisters send me velvet pieces, or quilt blocks. Will return favor with toy animal patterns.

A.L. REYNOLDS, Thrasher, Miss.

Miss Carrie Hoffman, Keystone, Nebr. would like June 1916 and 1917 numbers of the "Illustrated Companion." Will return favor.

Will someone please tell me what "California Beer Seeds" are, where they may be obtained, and how they are used.

A.B., New York, NY

I would be very glad if the readers of COMFORT would send me pages containing patterns and fancy work. Also used picture postcards of any kind.

MRS. C.F. RITCHEY, Center Point, Ark.

multiples of ten, how i loved the way we galloped :

                but i fell asleep in fields macadam-black, their sweating gutters : still

we prospered. i sent my sister an endless knot :

                      it got lost in the mail : too infinite for the system

is boiling lamps in water to make them stronger. is slipping her pancake turner under the pie & seldom burning her fingers. is filling her mouth with sassafras, very hot water for bruises. & when the water is bloodwarm put it in a quart glass jar with sugar & salt : wait in a warm place until evening : for what is home without a father

our children were raised
together   in
the same white box of a room

                of a fallen-in

                      lath accident

a ricochet version of time
a sink ratchet-mended

a porch bloomed
black with mold   an open-

-handed what

& i dreamt the space between my fingers

      was spring-loaded wool

      would carom the cracks away

is given a free breakfast table. is given a free homestead. is promised the latest patterns in exchange for five subscriptions. is warm mash in the morning. is opening up the hens postmortem—the eggs seem hard, as though they've been cooked. is drooping & drooping, refusing to eat. is scattering night across the floor of the house. is measuring happiness, by which i mean comfort : sinkwater running out gray : to the yard uncovered :

: *the colors i wear in the sun*   *the colors i was*   *in sun*   *worn* is moving through the poppies. is searching for trees like the ones back home : burdened with fruit : here only stars move on their own : no anchor, no time-telling : just slaughters to see by : o hull-motion. o that feeling of hundredfold birds, not heat / exhaustion / just *prairie as ocean* :

: a clean gone roof : a knock at the door : a drought : a seed body moving with boreal wind, unknowingly brought to a desert : a lovely country & the air is fine, but it's so new : there is nowhere to go tonight, for once : so be my little comforter

you planted a tree in my elbow crease

dawn was a deal between one day
& the next & i guess
the deal went bad

i never heard the bell ring but i saw the red-caped children

                                                                               rounding bends
                                                                               moving west

                             it's all some story you told me

supine
when i was grass

and you an insect
or you the sun & me cash
crop   (repetition

of *winterwheat*   *winterwheat*
under the rain)

                              : the kind of promise

                                 that makes ghosts

and the ocean shrank away from the plains *& timetables*

caramelized into layers & ships sailed passengerless & flags were torn

to shreds & the old ways died & a trance was woven between all folk

& they grew thinner & more alert & how i want to dance

but find my legs have been broken painlessly in the night

and some beings were brought
(in this false past)   to new pasture saying

      be with me and i will make hands
      out of zero i will make strong backs
      from this cold air if we lie together
      for a while,   be with me

soon sure enough small hands and backs
emerged from a thousand low red holes :

i've learned the things that haunt me

haunt nobody else. i am a shell
of a vehicle

only a blood-hum of peace

peace peace in winter
interior warm with colored life : our little   on the prairie

: *DAY* :

    : to part ways with hasps

to drill
into the wall, find wasps : find wasps'

                              nests underneath plaster

    : to eat berries out of a handkerchief   or from the well

        of fabric created with upturned

                              apron   purple

                          spreading in starlike patterns

            across a cartesian
            cotton grid

home feels like

several odd chunks that manage to fit
in the hand

: *good enough* :

(apple wagon, star, etc.)

we take on
room disguises

(you the foyer

      me the mudroom before you)

household notes

insects like neither
salt nor alum   hot
vinegar removes paint
stains from glass   clean a gold
chain with wood
alcohol   a fern with drooping
fronds is rootbound   boil
a rusty garment in cream
-of-tartar   polish flatirons with paraffin
paper   cold water for pain
of an inflamed eye   peach
halves filled with whipped
sweet cream   clean carpets
with finely-grated potato   polish
white shoes with starch and water   save
leftover fish in a fruit jar   darn socks
over a shoe tree   remove the skins
from all fruit to be eaten by children   stay
where you are   a change will be
of no benefit now

so i create a small space
where leaves can blow
across the road in summer

the ones that fall easy all
over themselves in a hurry
to get to the river :

that's where i hold you

that's my little death

that's the way afternoon

light hits the stairs

our clan wants for nothing
but a bowl that's not broken :

a whole one to sip from : solder me :

let me be an insect
on your inner
thigh, drop-leafed :

: a day-mote spinning in sunlight
        by the door jamb

        & tell me the west
        and east signs of my truly being here :

        stretched taut across consecutive fields :

        look down, daughter   [a voice]
        it's a maze in your navel
        come up in place of cord

is obscured by a strip of brittle yellow tape where air had entered the side of her head. is holding her hands in the air. is kneeling. is planted barefoot : arm-saggy, dough-eater : umbrella for her own existence. is stripes in the sun, stippled red. is staring. is certainly aging, but not as quickly as one might expect. is coveting pearls, even false ones. is hoisting the child to hip so that he is taller : someone's arm hooked to hers, always : hanging there bandaged from the plow. has an empire waist. is going to town with hot baskets & napkins laid over bread. does not have an apple barrel aesthetic. something appears on the floor she just washed, or maybe she'd missed it from the start :

crumbs of comfort

                        prevention

                    is the best bridle

                                    sorrows

                                      our spurs

he that sips daylight :

      they can conquer

who believe they can   the parent of doubt

                                                    the artful child

                                                  a heart of heated steel

                    the greatest secret of life is
                       to never be in the way :

is running a small piece of sand soap through the grinder. is dipping brooms in hot suds. is tying a cord around a glass stopper. is ending prairie dogs, gophers, ground hogs, weasels, squirrels, crows & hawks for good. is not dying in the house & smelling : is doing it outside in the breeze : is waiting for the barn to go up : holed front as face : embossed with botanicals : a question mark thinly entered, a fence (all maplines implying fence). is banks of snow that stayed white—nothing to stain them. is holding the child's hand as if birth in reverse. is the highest window, the one from which no face peered. is fallen : the hat slipped off, the naked curls on the ground. is false blue snakeskin, or its tint. is a pond filled with other people. is turning around at the sound of her name

some seeds germinate only with
their hulls charred open

but nobody talks about that

opening stitched with small leaves then
sewn shut with brambles   i become

light as what takes me here
slapped away and milked

for what all is good in you

you are dead   i am dying   therefore
we are separate

therefore we are in love

: is color on a longed-for hobby horse : is a tire holding water, a one-story tower : fleabane, bluestem : a knotted series, or is it a series of knots : is never on the floor : is a well getting low, water hauled bareback : is borrowing thread for the morning : for days : has a breast-pin, a pretty glass cup & a collar for presents : is clearing the carcasses, whipping butter across the knee with a clothesbrush : is always walked home by somebody new : was all ready to do the wash so she did but the wind (again) disregarded her pins

a porch repainted white, rain puddling on the steps. and when
the child comes it will be a saving. and when it's over the rainbow dissolves :

                                                      (i am actual space / red scatters across my field

                                                     of vision / begging to be shot / to be married

                                                     to a hole)

: no difference

between paint

and prism :

is a grass-filled track, a record. is timber & staff, the stuff of fairs. is a water tank filled with smoke, then snow. is a black wall battered with hailstones, booms & busts & strawberry pie & lines of work. is ice against glass, is tables suspended in air : a tea kettle, knotted hair. the dog at a set angle, always, on the rug

: a quick death, back to work : weather
appears in streaks, dashes
of seed down a stunted row : he

chose me for wits and hips : in making
the home we have made
many homes : prosperity clones : have planted

a tree for each birth

& when the little one fell down the stairs
a gray-purple stain appeared
on the waxed wood : innocence

impact : the way her wounds
capsule all bad, scab
up, renew so quick—

CURE FOR CORNS

Take a well-ripened lemon, roll and squeeze, then open one end into a glass vial. Add to the juice three or six pearl buttons (according to size) such as those used on cambric underwear. In a few days (it will be found) the lemon juice has eaten up the buttons, so they can be mashed between thumb and finger. Shake well. A few applications will conquer the most stubborn settler.

is fond of fancywork : goes over it twice. is a three-piece scissor set, purl or (fire) seam. is edge then space. is space then treble. is turning a (windstorm) thread over needle. is casting & binding (cyclone), omitting the narrowing (ice). is fastened off neatly. is slipping the first (tornado) stitch. is starting the row in the usual way : repeating & bracketed (is so plain) : blazing star, apple tree, goldenrod, sieve. is taking a minute to breathe before dinner & reading by gas : a blue wheel reflection, a mail order pattern : one : *cut here & tatter* : two : *if halo then* (weather) *revere* :

: i loved you so much this morning
i fed myself minutes of you

& questions of you

& your hair which is disappearing
& your beard which is disappearing

your eyes which are coming into being

& i asked you to tie
a red ribbon across
our bedroom doorway

instead you
undressed me :

: o love you are large

it mellows me out

warm   purpose but no expectation

                            dissection of the plane

that is my chest   a mail-order cure-all that comes

with a snap of my fingers   a sharp

                    in-draw of breath

but i don't stop

painting a room when

the walls are covered

—give me more credit than that

you drive :

acceptor
and / or
rejector

depending on the angle of the gesture

catenary : a chain
on a neck lies this way :

in a cosine swoop :

how tractors
avert rivers

is the blister-sheen of charcoal, coming down the road kicking floor-length skirt. is brushing dust from curios in the forest of overstuffed chairs : heat lightning, cast iron wristsprain : is filling bobbins with thread before starting to sew. is therefore saving time. is rubbing salt in her milk vessel, staying sweet. is making tea towels from old table linen. is bought by the yard & worn by the foot. is jellying chicken, disjointing & washing before removing from fire. is a single envelope of gelatin heated, set on ice until hard saying *please advise*

    then work a row

                      of loops, of preceding

                                                rows

next work   by ending row

                                  between rolls,

between the next two.

                repeat

                      all around. repeat all around

then work

                to center of

   work

                        a trefoil of roll

              picots   repeat till there are

                                                    twenty-two

turn work on

          back of central   roll

   repeat ending at end
   of row

                        just before
                cluster, repeat all across.

now work

              across the space left
              at the neck

then work :

then work :

now work :

is lining the interior with unbleached muslin. is tacking a line of pockets inside. is freshening feather pillows : without wringing, they are exactly right. is treating chapped hands with a thick salve of lard & flour applied at night. is confusing brining with burning. was afraid the dog had been killed but toward morning he was heard scratching at the door : a halo of silt in the sink : watered-silk in the attic : the need to wax : the cylinder itself. is mottled, is beetles killed with dish soap, diluted. is skirting the melting snow that clings to the housesides, as if cold lived there alone. is wall studs : either mold or a spirit collecting : is what is the meaning of : ownership, full, or nothing at all : is staying because sometimes a body doesn't know when to stop :

they say   she raised peacocks and grapes   against all advice

—women inherit the worst

slices of property :   abandoned graveyard,   only 2 arable acres,   etc.

i just kept pulling bones out of the ground

she said

      [the seer]

she couldn't grow what she set out to   and her field was a thicket of corpses

    because crazy means less acreage   wilderness cordoned   (the worst part

; the burial place, the old   we don't want to know)

as the gov't road widened   her property shrank   into an overgrown triangle is asking for a new oven. is writing away for one & away & away & after months receiving something underwhelming. is only two arms, only two hands & *there are limits to what i can do*. is laying out buttons of certain sizes (depending). is rolling a lemon across the counter with the heel of her hand. is removing stitches. is collecting pullets dead of the croup from the yard. is throwing glass bottles one at a time down the silo (reversed; in-ground). is waiting for the break. is glad for the distance. is tortured by distance. is asking each child to polish their own boots. is teaching some to do one sort of task, & the others another sort. is teaching herself the latest insertion. is going to town for calico. is going to town for green bone. is writing in to offer help. is efforting every day. is hard on her knees. is hard on her lumbar. is on top of her own fertility, mostly. is counting drops of chestnut oil, one for every year the child is old (for whooping cough). is seasoning sirup. is adding to her collection of patterns. is dissolving lye in rainwater. is covering her nose & mouth. is managing the lifespan of every species. is stewing & keeping. is keeping on top of. is managing loss. is consolidating. is cooking things that keep a full week, even in summer. is walking to the mailbox on w. 21 rd. & putting the red flag up. is walking the access. is walking the property's perimeter over & over squeezing between the ditch & the fence & saying *this cadaster is bramble scratches, this cadaster is feet-made ruts*

i was cloudless

sky crowded
by gnats

i was sun

in the eyes of a stranger
but red is no longer

the only color
and red is not

the only
section of light

(warm beneath an orb)

                                            hold me there
                                            to that

trainsound

tree shadows
on our bedroom blinds

                                          if only the dead
                                          could know this

you were standing there : holding my hand to the wax : i was holding in my other : multiple hands a range of remedies and chemicals : the liquids eating away their containers : artifice dropping into the natural : blending there : something forming and i was still standing : toe cramping : doling out advice (you transcribing with a hunk of lead) : bucket-handles rutting my forearms : red lines : divots : standing in sleep like a horse : milk pouring down from the eaves : and i said (or was it she) :

beware this warm grip   *for i live in the brown space*
    between generations   *where all is resolved*

was walking home one night when i said *why* *of course that's it*

for everyone wants comfort

: *DUSK* :

v.

1. to be native to a specific region
2. to make level or even
3. to arrange in a certain order; esp. in a row or rows
4. to put into the proper class or classes
5. to travel over or through; roam about [to *range* the prairie]
6. to move along parallel to [to *range* the river]
7. to put out (cattle, etc.) to graze on a range
8. to uncoil (e.g. the cable of an anchor) and arrange on deck (e.g. of p. schooner)
9. to extend, reach, or lie in a given direction [hills *ranging* toward the west]
10. to roam through an area, as in hunting [dogs *ranging* through the woods]
11. to vary between stated limits [children *ranging* in age from 5 to 12]
12. to be projected a certain distance [a call that *ranges* half a mile from the house]

n.

1. the full extent over which something moves or is heard, seen, or understood
2. the full extent of pitch, from highest to lowest tones, of a voice

[so that the word *deranged* implies an exile]

i remembered to cover up the mound today. began my ambulatory, stopped

        at the pile of bones i've seen so many times i don't see it anymore.

and the fire opened the pine cone, the boiling water opened the mouth of the shell

        the feet and hands tangled together in a victual net

the other day wandering

    i saw a shape at property's edge :

        the seer
    effigy in her pocket
    baby on her hip

    from all the way over there she somehow told me

    you

    will conquer those
    who would do you harm

she
moved
her
entire
body
like
a tongue

    if you tell your snake dream

she somehow said

    you will quarrel
    with the person to whom you told it

is making a morning of wrong moves. is heather hung out to dry. is sleeping in the same room as the stove. is putting a wet finger to the wind. is wiping sirup from small but growing hands. is growing eyes in the back of her head. is the outer eye opening inner. up with the sun : hedge fence about the black cherries. is patterned planting. is the orchard quincunx. is stopping after the second form : coming home to be married : troweling a circle of sprouts from a heart-rotted oak. is accused of killing her own :

firstborn locates
the pages : buttery folds of mildew in the fifth chapter : a crinkle or two, but
what does this have to do with

                                              counter-question : where did the storm originate

                      i think i know a fire
         under the hood

                                      death howl   penance

                    i am wild in the belly but

this single body can't replicate historical sound

                                 a scratch of sun :
                                 let the glass fall
                                 in pieces onto the road

                               bear a bouquet of wire
                               fragments to me,   my wonder

                        i live with you inside
                              wheat   we were first

           symbols
           next paintings
           finally   we are maquettes of our time

we are other people's dark age

when i kiss you   is it someone
later's laugh

smelled the day grow long & rot :

the length of a day in a place

                      where suns are lateral : blue moths

leap inside fire. both doors open and shut :

                           both doors placate the thresher. both doors open

on pockmarked breasts & i rolled over

                    a new length of bone poking out of the ground, rolled over

a wheel & spoke *are there hairs below dirt that have still not dissolved* :

is loving the land's enigma. is listening to coyote calls layered with other sound : coyote with rain, coyote with buzz-saw bug high up in the poplar, coyote with combine. is kneeling in the floating barn, picking through owl pellets. is separating fluff with her fingers, feeling for vole bones, stowing them in a tea tin for someone years later to ask herself *why*

all it is

is a way to cope :

i reckon you

my partner in dust :

ask after me, ask

after me all

of your days :

and i move
On—the place not Here

                (uneven
           showerhead of summer)

days fell
into the pond

i related

to you
the places i'd been
sketching them out
in smoke

rings   (an exit)

i will take you to a wide sea
some day : smooth glass

from green bottles : necklaces
for you : our animals dragging

their hind legs backward through
mud, up from the oil :

                    all is over

: the horses
gone by morning

           take the space between

           my hands & fill it with waste

                          the blister made by rubbing me
                          reaches capacity here :

    on the radio
a retelling of our nation's story

         a motionless fruit
hoisted over the square &
up the flagpole   starting to turn

                          (*these bullet silos*)

is speaking from the rock, is looking through the hole, is colors of lake foam, clear black ice. the river recedes, clouds of ash cover the field but the corn keeps growing : snow will come : she buries herself in stalks : ribbons that reach through the dark to run up her legs, criss-cross, balletic, alone for some hours in the house. ribbons of darkest brown : smooth : like the rim of a horse's eye

rolling hill
of the body's
cold forelegs :

you are a child
hemorrhaging me

                                          [*the growing hedge is useless*

                                                              for some years, during which time it needs

                                                        protection for itself]

i've come too close to leave my pasture
full of investments behind

i'm waiting for sound to stop :

always take a newborn baby upstairs before you take him downstairs, otherwise you'll incline him downwards for life : tomorrows in jars lined up in the cellar : everything moves sooner or later, even the fence

        ate the barn-yard's
        wild onions alone

now i have subjectivity &   you have nothing

    i tried to share the bed   hanging by chain
    from the wraparound porch—

but the sun will keep you

    company : i'll cut you a third
    eyelid : then you'll see

    my adoration plain
    as morning : plain
    as the mess of hair

    you culled from the setter

the seer

in a pile

by the silo   i swear :

evenings at the window :   the same

window i'm looking out of :

            so how—

                        she somehow tells me   *when i was a child a snake*
                                                licked my ears clean & now i can truly hear

                        she uses each limb as perimeter : spreads

the whole of her skin across our portion of sky   handing me chicory

[she is chicken wire casting

            thinnest crossed shadows

into my hands]

                                    now i'm sleeping in outbuildings : corncrib

                        lettered with message :

carry rattles   around the neck

about the ankle   between the breasts & make

a circle of rope around you :

            coil it like a snake

is fire : a glow from the front, from inside the burn barrel, chain of silos lit up from behind : horizon-bound black column : walking the road, no shoes as something beyond her flowers in orange tunnels : a bombed-out swamp, a prairie dog splayed, a swarm of attic locusts. is a weather pattern, a sweater pattern, a stripping : red fruit, tent-given : is revival, thereby explosion. town buildings low & flat below cumuli, distaff blue : her youngest opens the door, hangs off the knob in footies, cupping his ear complaining : she holds out only one hand, the other being immersed in boiling water :

a makeshift place to hold the fire, a mysticized study of pain :

                    sun disappears but the song stays, the heat stays : severity

of how you see me : the love, somehow, of a life : a life

                                  in which we look for lost objects : in which

    the last lost objects belong to us

i don't ask you anymore
to stay here   i release you to the goblet of coming night

where it sits on stilts
leaned up against the barn

you would come up
            meet me at the quarry

whereupon i would change
into a creature you could trap with paper

        & then we would hold
our bones together

you would flay roots
        if it brought you (here)

                (to this woody center; me)

        to the corona, a blue
        ring of coin-eating machines (my mouths)

is the wheel. is a single loop. is creekside lupine. is scarification, is skin ballooned, is wings on the roof. a sow seen from below as only teats. a row of corn then soy then corn. a sheen of rain on brick. is puddle, is moon, a parachute in : a centrifuge : cream from milk, water from clothes. is apron (endless belt for carrying things) : strings in the back, ocean of white in the front, clean start. is clumps of sorrel along the river. is always looking for more, beating the rugs, slipping on rungs, tenderly gripping her own wrists : always : holding the chasms closed :

watched a fire jump the break, opened the window

                to black exhaust.   cooked a meal forward and backward. without

urgency scraped   the crumbs onto the floor, made a paste of the crumbs

                      and the walls' condensation, applied it

      to the lock on your door :

IF A LAMP SHOULD BE OVERTURNED

Remember that water spreads the flames. Milk may be used to extinguish them, but the best things to throw down are sand, earth, and flour.

is the strapdown, the braid down the back because practical (also pretty). is at the vanity. is losing value. is posing but not smiling. is damage come in the form of water. is wrinkle, dusk, no fight in her. is a burn, a hexagonal pen, a joyful accident : is molded according to patterns of light & exposure : is red seeping up from the bottom, a shaft of light, an early harvest. is fingers coming through wool. is never a good sign. is prints in the silt & no boots in the house. is baths in the sink. is keeping the inside clean, even with all the cracks & wind. is an open-palmed gesture directed at sky. is ash & breakers of grass & rope. is electric come to the county : finally : reed-shadows, warblers, bee balm & chiggers : an upturned horseshoe holding good luck. is a peeling corner of tar, is rot, is something welded to itself. is blazing purely with sound :

: at the water pump, in prevailing winds, with divining rods but no lightning rod because god's will, water pump, peg lock. is sliding out from the wall to keep horses in, going to feed them at four in a rainstorm, a hay bay, a barn bay, a grain-bin, a full fore-bay, a straw-room, a false breast-wall, a saddle-notch, a borning stall, going to birth them at two in a snowstorm, a turnip room, an assignation, a spring house, a glassless transom, a smoke house, a sugar camp, a corncobbed floor, a rug burn, a wet cellar, a peak, a weathervane, a moon-shaped cutout to indicate women, *window* from *wind-eye*, for where it comes through & can see i can't

stay here

there was a list of the ways & i read it to you

       outside the shelterbelt

       at the property line

       in the purple room of dusk :

i can only say
there is what you know &

what i know & those things may never

converge
in the field i want them to

              (and here a worn
              ottoman interrupting the perfect
              length of the rug)

elsewhere-languages
spoken in the ell

light shines butter-crass on
blue snow

            question (crumbling) : whether men
            or women make better choices

& you find an extra fold of space
in the pocket of world

& label it
me & this : calm eyes
when you tell me about the frame
around our pocket-world : the net

worth of my actions :
nothing & i am the last
one to swallow the earth

in this house : a hard clod : empty

the hands the sockets the

mouth of all

hope ; i'll catch up with you later

so some things just don't go anywhere

they fall to the side of the purple road

i walk in a scarf line through untold

color and i can

forgive myself

milk poured on graves,   nails baked in cakes,   root-nosed knotted light in the
        pines in the pines a blank space in the fabric of fields
                              reflective   accruing sweet   rose-scented
sachet   muddy boots sit by the door, wing inward. we don't

        talk about somethings
      parlay the rent into mortgage   slap a tall branch   into dress bones

can name some, o but only the type.   clicks
                      in the ear let it be
      wrinkled   astringent to the taste but rather

    agreeable
        ripples & accrues & doesn't care
                      for screens in the door.   islands in the

prairie / ocean

            if comfort's been here all this time

and continues
        a curtain in wind   not controlled

only taken,
    don't lie to me / tell me

            where did you sleep last night :

& sing me

a way of being
close to me
without being
inside me

my blue self is
quiet and waiting
for my red half
to return

                                           but you won't slow down to see

                                           death's purple mergings   you won't see

                                           a new life for the field

                                           each season the ditch deepens :

                                           an undertow in a stone
                                         room :

                                         steeped in burning
                                         lavender :

lock yourself out

once
                i'll let you in
twice
                [*i can't do this anymore*]

                                       everything is change in the valley of summer :

                                       the conflagration is me

if you love this body let it go into sedge

into bluestem in search of   tall ships   and their anchors.   anchors

hold down the roof of our house,   oxidized

prisms that mimic

true north. & a ways out

                          i watch the blonde
                          wood get relief
                          from the winter
                          sun as it sets :

                                                please leave me here to heal

                                        leave me here wanting more

                                        in a circle of purple sky

                                           in the circle we built together :

i turn on the light   & living things

scamper off the world's edge

let it be let it be   sings the one that stays behind   [but i smell the wind]

: this is the proximal book :

a dream in which we grow long

joints swollen

easily by weather

this is a vision of the last page :

blame the rust but that is change

: strain / cover / keep :

this has never been known to fail

ACKNOWLEDGMENTS

Comfort would not exist without the work of Pattie McCarthy. I am indebted especially to her book *Marybones*, which directly inspired the form of this book's prose blocks. Thank you for showing me new ways to work with found language and the historical record.

Neither would it exist without my teachers at San Francisco State University, in whose classes I developed the manuscript: Maxine Chernoff, Donna de la Perrière, Andrew Joron, Toni Mirosevich, Barbara Tomash, and Truong Tran. Thank you for bringing me the texts that brought this text into being, and for helping me shape a four-hundred-page pile of fragments into a book.

Endless gratitude to the editors at Spuyten Duyvil, who believed fiercely in *Comfort* and and in my vision for its physical presence. Thank you for so deeply seeing this work.

Clare Rojas generously allowed me the use of one of her paintings for the book's cover—a dream come true. Thank you for making images that fueled the writing of *Comfort* by so perfectly articulating the strangeness at the heart of desire.

Jennifer S. Cheng and Tanya Holtland taught me patience and walked me through the darkness in which I found this book. Thank you for your hearts and your accompaniment.

Margie, Eli, and Maia Ipp lent me their apartment to write in while they were out of town. Thank you for the gifts of space, time, and a sublime view.

Lauren Peck told me about grapes and peacocks and the subpar agricultural tracts that get passed on to women. Thank you for sharing where you came from.

Leah Virsik (under the guidance of Mario Laplante) made *Tatted Insertion*, a limited edition letterpress artist's book that came from the world of *Comfort*. Thank you for helping me build that world.

Shmee Giarratana, Patty Pforte, Martha Schwarz, and Arielle Tonkin helped me think through land acknowledgment. Thank you for holding me accountable.

My beloved, Joseph Crockett, posited that there is "a kind of promise that makes ghosts." Thank you for your promise, and for being my home.

The following people are also part of the story of this book: the Asylum Arts Bay Area crew, Rachelle Axel, Amy K. Bell, Amy Berkowitz, my work family at California Institute of Integral Studies (especially Carolyn Cooke, Danielle Freiman, Emlyn Guiney, and Charles Wilmoth), the Castro Writers' Cooperative, Leora Fridman, Emily Hale, Melinda and Paul Heady, Hailey Higdon, Jill Tomasetti, and Heidi Van Horn. Thank you all for your steadfast support.

I owe a very special thank you to Ed Dadey of Art Farm in Marquette, Nebraska. Ed let me root around in the attic of the farmhouse where he was born, and it was there I found the copies of *Comfort* magazine that brought this project together. Undoubtedly, it was also through him that the story of Susan Gavan, the "Aurora Witch," was passed to the artists-in-residence of Art Farm. Her grave stands alone in the cemetery of Aurora, Nebraska, and she served as the inspiration for my seer.

Marquette and Aurora are both located on the ancestral lands of the Pâri (Pawnee) Nation, which is based in the place now called Oklahoma following the tribe's forced expulsion from the place now called Nebraska in the mid-1870s. Peoples of the Great Sioux Nation (Očhéthi Šakówin, or Seven Council Fires) also occupied this part of Nebraska after being driven from their own territories by other tribes, in a cascading series of pressurizing events caused by white colonization.

Comfort centers the experiences of white women who, through their settlement, participated in the genocide and displacement of the Pâri, the Očhéthi Šakówin, and other tribes of the Great Plains and the Midwest. In her book *Upend* (Noemi Press, 2020), poet Claire Meuschke articulates the fallout that such participation can generate:

19th century colonial women / suffered nationally a leg paralysis / Western science called it psychosis / what about immobilizing guilt / organized resistance / the land not wanting you?

Coming across this passage several years after writing *Comfort*, I was struck by how the underlying condition of settler colonialism explains so much of the emotional landscape (*un*settledness, *dis*comfort) suggested by my book. I want to make this explicit here, now, as the book itself may not do so. This is because I placed my emphasis on patriarchy rather than on racial capitalism—though these two are, of course, inextricable. Claire's words startled me into a new kind of knowing, and this knowing filled me with shame: a hollowed-out feeling of doubt that *Comfort* should even exist. Perhaps that is good.

But we know that shame doesn't help us contribute or repair anything. It doesn't enable humility, compassion, or service; it keeps us stuck and silent. And so:

If you enjoyed *Comfort*, please consider donating to the Pawnee Seed Preservation Society, which is reclaiming Pawnee cultural sovereignty by restoring the tribe's traditional foodways, centered around heritage varieties of corn but including other crops like beans, pumpkin, squash, watermelon, and sunflower. These foodways were almost lost to extinction during the tribe's exile from Nebraska to Oklahoma, but a small seed bank preserved by tribal elders over generations has allowed them to flourish again under the guidance of Deb Echo-Hawk, Pawnee Keeper of the Seeds, since 1998.

You can learn more at facebook.com/pawneeseedpreservationsociety and prairiecitizen.com/culture/pawnee-reclaim-their-sacred-corn-and-sacred-history, and you can donate via check mailed to:

Pawnee Seed Preservation Society
46200 S. 34700 Road
Pawnee, OK 74058

Or find another organization that speaks to you at Native Owned & Operated (ndnoando.com/nonprofits). The (non-Native-led) Prairie Plains Resource Institute (prairieplains.org), based in Aurora, restores prairie ecosystems across Nebraska and also welcomes your support. And if you would like to learn whose ancestral lands you live on, please visit Native Land Digital (native-land.ca).

NOTES

Comfort magazine was published in Augusta, Maine between 1888 and 1942. Its tagline was "The Key to Happiness and Success in Over a Million Farm Homes." Aimed at rural housewives, it began as a thinly-veiled vehicle for selling Oxien, a cure-all snake oil, with subscribers receiving discounts and bonus gifts for signing up their female friends—perhaps an early multi-level marketing scheme. At the same time, it provided a valuable source of virtual companionship for women who led isolated lives all across the United States. Much of the found language in this book comes from issues of *Comfort* published in the 1910s and 1920s.

In addition, the following texts either made their way directly into the book or floated in the background as I wrote:

Ossian Brown, Geoff Cox, and David Lynch, *Haunted Air*
Edwin A. Curley, *Nebraska 1875: Its Advantages, Resources, and Drawbacks*
William Gabler, *Death of the Dream: Classic Minnesota Farmhouses*
Kay Graber, ed., *Nebraska Pioneer Cookbook*
John Brinckerhoff Jackson, *Discovering the Vernacular Landscape*
William Least Heat-Moon, *Blue Highways* and *PrairyErth*
H. Elaine Lindgren, *Land in Her Own Name: Women as Homesteaders in North Dakota*
Frederick C. Luebke, *Nebraska: An Illustrated History*
Susan Griffin, *Woman and Nature: The Roaring Inside Her*
Louise Pound, *Nebraska Folklore*
Marilynne Robinson, *Lila*
Dorothy Steward Sayward, *Comfort Magazine, 1888-1942: A History and Critical Study*
Eric Sloane, *An Age of Barns*

Jane Smiley, *A Thousand Acres*

Marlene & Haskell Springer, eds., *Plains Woman: The Diary of Martha Farnsworth, 1882-1922*

John R. Stilgoe, *Common Landscape of America, 1580 to 1845*

J.E. Weaver, *Native Vegetation of Nebraska*

Webster's New World Dictionary of the American Language, Second College Edition

William Wyckoff, *How to Read the American West*

Sarah Heady is a poet and essayist interested in place, history, and the built environment. She is the author of *Corduroy Road* (dancing girl press, 2021); *Niagara Transnational* (Fourteen Hills, 2013), winner of the 2013 Michael Rubin Book Award; and *Tatted Insertion* (2014), a limited edition letterpress chapbook with artist Leah Virsik. Sarah is also the librettist of *Halcyon*, a new opera about the death and life of a women's college, in collaboration with composer Joshua Groffman and producer Vital Opera. She is the recipient of residencies and fellowships from the Corporation of Yaddo, Asylum Arts, In Cahoots, the Home School, Art Farm, and Summer Literary Seminars. Raised in the Hudson River Valley of New York State, she now lives in San Francisco, where she co-edits Drop Leaf Press, a small women-run poetry collective. More at sarahheady.com.

www.ingramcontent.com/pod-product-compliance
Lightning Source LLC
Chambersburg PA
CBHW051806100526
44592CB00016B/2592